# 21 DAYS TO LAUNCH

"An Entrepreneurs, Course Creators, Coaches and Consultants
Guide to Growing Their Business Online in 21 Days"

By Daniel Steed

Daniel Steed

21 Days to Launch.

© 2019, Daniel Steed

Self-published

info@socialonpoint.com

Once upon a time, an online coach went fishing to pass the time,

He sat down, prepared his hook, attached the bait and cast his best line,

8 hours pass and nothing to report, not one bit of interest,

"I best be on my way home" he said, "tomorrow might be different".

And then a man appeared on the other side and shouted, "HEY STOP FISHING FOR CLIENTS!"

"What? The coach replied. The man yelled "I SAID, STOP FISHING FOR CLIENTS!"

The coach not hearing him correctly... "Who's got a robin reliant?"

The man getting annoyed and thinks why the coach is not being compliant.

The man on the other side is wondering what the coach's purpose is.

"NO... I MEAN WRITE YOUR OWN BOOK SO PEOPLE TRUST YOU WHICH MEANS THEY'LL FLOOD YOUR SERVICES..."

"Ah, it's not going to rain today don't worry..." The Coach not taking it in

"Anyway, I'll be back tomorrow, see ya later!" Now the Coach not knowing what could have been...

### *Dedication*

*This book is dedicated to my family who have always believed in me and to people like Frank Kern, Russell Brunson, Jim Edwards and Franklin Hatchett who have shown me the way to growing an online business.*

# TABLE OF CONTENTS

# Introduction

It was back in 2018, I was 28 and working in a care home for Children just outside Shrewsbury, England. The birthplace of Charles Darwin, the man who discovered the theory of relativity – you know the theory you only tell your relatives. (sorry, Red Dwarf joke)

So, around this time, I went through a tough time with the kids who were abusing me in all sorts of ways. I was getting spat at, kicked, punched and nearly stabbed on a few occasions. The whole time I was thinking, "why am I doing this to myself?"

While working in the care system, it was tough, not just the abuse you get from kids, but the staff turnover rate was ridiculous. I was often having to stay on shift because someone did not want to face the abuse again.

I was only supposed to do 2 x 24 hour shifts a week but now I am doing at least 5 – that's 120 hours a week minimum. When I would come off shift, I would just stay in bed until I had to go back and do it all again. It was a never-ending cycle and it finally broke me.

I know I really do care about these kids and the stuff they went through was horrific, but I deserve better than this – these kids deserved better. So, I was stuck between a rock and a hard place – wondering what I should do. Do I selflessly try to make these kids' lives a bit better or do I try and find my calling?

I did what all the other staff did – I pulled a sickie to find my future – I looked online for possible career changes and I came across Franklin Hatchett, a Youtuber who teaches Affiliate Marketing – this is where you promote a product in exchange for a commission. He said for you to be successful in Affiliate Marketing or anything online is to build an email list so you can continue to sell products and services to people for years to come through email marketing.

I thought, yes that sounds perfect – I do not have to create anything. So, I bought his course and studied everything I needed to know. And the first thing I did was I created a blog where I would have lots of articles promoting certain products to make affiliate commissions. But I did not want to write the articles as I was pretty lazy, so I got a loan out of £3,000 to pay people to write blog articles for me. Within 30 days, I had 100 blog articles at 2,500 words a piece.

To put it bluntly... they were utter dog shit... I had to go through it all and proofread everything – lots of it did not make sense. I thought great, what a waste of money that was! I did not even finish proof-reading them – there still some on this hard drive that need editing –

maybe one day, I will do it or pay someone to do it. Anyway, going off track here.

So, after those articles were published, I started to panic. My sick note was about to run out and I was nowhere near to making an income so I could quit the care home.

So, I did what any desperate person would do, I went to Facebook and started throwing the last of my money at Paid Ads hoping it would get me out of jail – I sent a bunch of traffic to my affiliate products and to cut a long story short, it did not work.

I had to return to work and my heart sank – I was so miserable. I was so sure this was going to be my escape from this life. A couple of weeks returning to work, I went on a rare night out in Birmingham. I had a few beers and sometime after midnight, I left everyone to wonder around the city centre in the dark.

I was so lost, and I did not know what to do - I found a bridge and I just wanted to jump off. Thankfully, I stopped myself after thinking about what it would do to my family and friends. So, I stepped off and returned to my mates where I bawled my eyes out.

Now suicide and mental illness is a big deal and if you ever feel the way I did, then please talk to someone – it really does help having people around you give you what you need.

Ever since that moment, I saw clarity and I was able to build myself back up piece by piece. So, after a few months working in the home and the shift patterns were getting slightly better, I decided to have another go at making money online.

This time, I decided I am going to have a strategy – I am going to create a product that will pay for my advertising allowing me to grow my email list so I can make affiliate commissions through email marketing.

So, I created a video course around the D.I.Y. niche and those sales would pay for my ads while growing my email list. After a month or so, I started seeing money trickle into my account – finally there was light at the end of the tunnel.

Every day, it would gradually get bigger and bigger to the point it started to outdo the wage I was making at the care home – I finally cracked it! So, I handed in my notice and I started working from home.

I started looking at the different affiliate products that paid more commissions and put more money into that. It grew and grew, and I finally achieved financial freedom. I was able to travel around the world and enjoy what life has to offer.

I got so good at Facebook Ads, that I decided to open my Social Media Marketing Agency Social on Point so I could help people like me achieve what they deserve.

Starting Social on Point was the best thing I have ever done because it has allowed me to see the difference I am making in people's lives - by helping people navigate the online world and help them reach their true potential makes me so proud.

Many entrepreneurs who use my services did the same exact thing when they first started out. They chucked a load of money at ads in the hope it would stick but they would fail.

Which brings me onto why am I writing this book?
The catalyst for writing this book was when a client wanted to speak to me because his Facebook Ads were not getting him sales, so he was not very happy – we had taken over his ads account for just a week at that point.

I explained to him, for paid ads to work, we need to test the market to see which ads resonate the best with his audience – this was explained to him at the time when he signed up through our onboarding system. (the onboarding system allows us to get as much information about their product and audience as possible so we can fulfil the order and not have to go back and forth with the client)

He then later admitted that he did not fill in our onboarding system correctly because he did not know who his audience was – he did not even know if there was a market. His mentality like mine when I first started was chuck enough money at a problem and it will fix itself.

That is when it hit me.

I needed to teach people how to find their audience first so they can build the foundations for their business which allows Social on Point to scale it for them quickly.

And that is the reason why I am writing this book. I want to provide such amazing value to my clients and potential clients that they will continue to use Social on Point and refer us to all their friends.

So, as I was writing the meat and potatoes of the book, I did not know what to call it – originally it was going to be called "Find Your

Audience." but as I was writing, I felt like I was holding a lot of value back, so I scrapped the idea and decided to incorporate Social on Point's paid strategies in here as well.

And this is where 21 Days to Launch was born.

Now, the steps I have laid out are a guide for you to follow – it depends on your work ethnic on how fast you get it done. It can take you 21 days, or it can take you 21 weeks – it is entirely up to you on how fast you want to progress.

However, the best advice I can give to people right now who are starting from scratch is to "don't worry about getting it perfect right now – just start right now and perfect it later. Build the foundations now, so you can reap the rewards after."

So, as we go along, I shall lay out some tasks for you to do on each day, so you have something to work on – please put 100% into this because it will only benefit you, agreed? Good, let us dive into launching your online Business, shall we?

# Day 1

## Where's your head at?

As you know when I first started my online journey, I rushed into it far too quickly without really knowing what I was doing – all I knew was I wanted to make money – that is all I really thought about.

But what really changed it for me that allowed me to start making money was getting in touch with what is going on in my head.

"Why did I want to make money?"

What are the reasons that make me want to make money? Why? By just wanting money in my mind, it was like tunnel vision – it did not allow me to open new thought processes so I could see the bigger picture.

Once I started asking myself why and holding myself accountable that is when I started to see success – not just financially but mentally and emotionally – I am a happier man for it.

So here is my thought process of holding myself accountable.

## Question:

*"Why do you want to start an online business?"*

## Answer:

*"Because I want to make more money."*

*"Why?"*

*"Because I hate my job at the care home."*

*"Why?"*

*"Because I feel undervalued, and I want to achieve more."*

"Why?"

"Because if I don't, then I'll always be seen as a loser and a failure."

"Why?"

"Because I want to make my mum and gran proud."

"Why?"

"Because I want to give back to them what they gave to me when they raised me."

"Why?"

*"Because I don't want to be a failure and lose everyone I love."*

You see, how I went from just wanting more money to opening about the fear of losing everyone I love.

By going through this thought process, I was able to accept things for what they are, and it allowed me to have clarity to pursue the things I knew I deserved. You must go through the same thought process if you want to achieve success financially, emotionally, mentally and even spiritually.

By doing this, I no longer have days where I crawl out of bed and wish I could just stay in it all day – no, every day I literally hop out of bed eager to achieve everything I want.

**<u>Task</u>**
**Find out what is going on in your head right now – ask yourself this question.**
***"Why do you want to start an online business?"***
**and hold yourself accountable by asking yourself why every time until you find the source of your pain.**

# Day 2

## Finding Your Avatar

So, now we understand ourselves better, we can then get into the mindset of the customers and clients we want to use for our products and services. Getting this day right is so important for your business to survive. If you do not know who or where your dream customer is then how are you going to attract those people - you need to get into the mindset of your dream customer.

## Creating Your Avatar

We can do this by creating an avatar that symbolises everything our Dream Customer is. For example, when I started Social on Point, my avatar was called F.R.E.D. (Fears, Results, Expectations and Desires).

"Fred is 45, speaks English, lives in America and runs a Consulting business - Fred is worried because he isn't getting any new clients and needs a solution fast. He is considering using Facebook Ads to acquire leads for his business but his experience from using the platform has not been good - Fred wants someone to take control of his social media to bring in lead after lead so he can have more freedom to focus on his consulting business and have more time to spend with his family - Fred wants my Social Media Marketing Services".

Once you can picture who your avatar is and understand their wants and needs then it allows you to position yourself as their authority figure.

### Task

**Write down your statement to find out who your Avatar is.**

# Two Types of Person

Next up we need to identify what kind of person they are. There are two types of people who want to achieve something that will make their lives better.

In Russell Brunson's book Traffic Secrets, he says that "every human being on this planet is moving in one of two directions when they make a decision: away from pain or towards pleasure."

# Moving Away from Pain

People moving away from pain are the type of people want to escape their struggles and worries.

- "My Consulting business is struggling, and I feel like I'll go out of business."
- "I hate talking on the phone which makes me feel uncomfortable closing deals".
- "I'm spending too much time finding clients and not spending enough time with my family."

## Moving Towards Pleasure

People moving towards pleasure are the types of people who are happy with what they already have but still want to improve certain aspects of their life.

- "I want to scale my business to make more money".
- "I want more time to spend with my family".
- "I want my company to make a difference and have more impact".

The reason why we need to look at these two types of people is so we can market to them with two different approaches but still get them the same results.

### Task
**Write down at least 10 statements for each type of person (the more the better). Over time, you want to keep adding to your list as you continue to know more and more about your avatar.**

18

# Where is Your Avatar?

To find our Avatar, we need to go to the places where they are currently congregating - these are called our Dream 100. Chet Holmes popularised the term in his book in detail, *The Ultimate Sales Machine*. Your Dream 100 are the people, sites and groups who already have your Avatar - our aim is to get in-front of these people and bring them back to us.

**Task - Answer these questions to find out your Dream 100. Write down as many as possible and continue to add to them as time goes on.**

1. What websites does my avatar go to?
2. What Facebook Groups are they active in?
3. Who are they following on Facebook and Instagram?
4. What Podcasts are they listening to?
5. What blogs do they read?
6. What YouTube Channels are they subscribed to?
7. What Keywords are they searching for on Google?
8. What Forums/Message-boards are they active in?
9. What Email Newsletters are they receiving?

By answering these questions, you will start to find out where your avatar is. Once you have got your list, add altogether the number of subscribers, followers, listeners etc and you can work out how many people you could potentially get for your business.

Next up, you want to follow and subscribe to all your Dream 100. The reason being is that we can analyse how their posts, offers, products and how their engage with their audience so we can model our approach around theirs.

In the future, we want to leverage our Dream 100 so we can be seen by their followers and be able to bring them back to us.

From day one, we need to like, comment and react to their posts and stories so that when we do come to talk to them, they will know who we are and be more inclined to message us back - if you do not plant the seed first then the chances of getting a reply is low.

### Task
**Follow and Interact with your Dream 100 daily.**

By identifying who our avatar is and where they are then it allows us to build the foundations to our business. When we get to our paid advertising to scale our business in the future then we will know exactly who and where to target which will save us thousands of dollars on ad spend.

# Day 3

## Biggest Asset

One of the biggest things that stuck with me from learning about Affiliate Marketing from Franklin Hatchett is the importance of having an email list – it is our way of making a passive income and our back up plan.

There is a common belief that Email Marketing is dead and pointless. "Who reads emails anymore?" Well, I and most people making money online will tell you it is their Biggest Asset. By collecting someone's email address, it allows us to build a relationship with that person so when we do emails, they will trust our recommendations, offers and promotions – the great thing is we do not have to pay to advertise to them again once we have acquired their email address thus saving us money.

Another important thing to consider when having an email list is it is your insurance policy. If you have an audience already and not collecting emails for your business, then you are making a massive mistake - you are putting you and your business at risk by not doing so. Let us say, you have an audience on Facebook and then one day, the unthinkable happens, your account gets deleted which means you have lost everyone and everything.

The problem with Social Media like Facebook and Instagram is that you do not own anything - you are only renting the space and Facebook is the landlord that can kick you out at any time.

What you need is a backup plan - you need to start collecting your audiences email addresses right now so that in case it does happen, you can just email your audience about your new platform, so you do not have to start from scratch.

Now with Social Media, such as Facebook for example, the content is filtered so much that it requires you to boost a lot of your posts to get any reach however with email marketing, it is up to 40 times more effective and the buying process is 3 times faster than in social media, according to a study done by McKinsey & Company.

So, email marketing is so important for growing and nurturing your audience which allows you to scale it quickly.

## How to Collect Email Addresses?

To start collecting email addresses, you need to have certain systems in place that allows you to capture details, store them and send automated emails to them once they sign up.

First thing you need to create is a Lead Magnet - this is something we give away for free in exchange for their information such as an email address/mobile number. Lead Magnets can be Free Training, an e-book, a cheat-sheet, a free consultation, etc. If it is solving a problem people have and it contains value, then give it away for free to get email addresses.

Once you have created your Lead Magnet, you then want to create a landing webpage with an opt-in form – this is where the lead will put in their details. On the page you will a headline to entice them to download your Lead Magnet so you can collect their email Address.

When people opt-in to your lead magnet, they are then sent to a "thank you page" where you explain to them that their freebie has been sent to their inbox - these two pages together are commonly known as a Lead Generation Funnel. On the "thank you page", you want to have the product or service you are selling or promoting or direct them in the direction of your private Facebook group. (More on that tomorrow)

The Lead Generation Funnel is fantastic for Organic traffic and should be placed in your Facebook Group, your website, pop ups, your Instagram Bio, etc.

This type of funnel can be used for paid ads, but the problem is you are not going to make your money back straight away as you must rely on your email marketing to do its magic. Spoiler: Later in the book, I shall show how to expand on this Funnel, so it pays for your advertising allowing you to scale quickly.

## Email Marketing

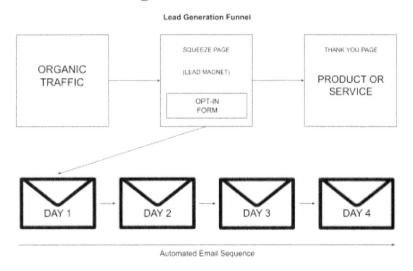

Lead Generation Funnel

Now you might be wondering where the emails you collect go to - they go into your email marketing tool and this is where you can program an email sequence to send to your email list automatically.

When someone signs up to your email list, we want to program at least 5 days of emails – the reason why we send 5 emails is that studies suggest that for someone to make a purchase on a product or service, they need to see the offer at least 5 times, hence 5 emails.

The 5-day email template goes like this:

**Day One:** The first email they get is the delivery of their lead magnet - in this email we need to introduce ourselves and tell them what they are going to expect from you in the future so we can start to build trust with our lead. Then, you want to end your email with a cliff-hanger, so they must read tomorrow's email.

**Day Two:** In the second email, you want to tell your story on what life was like before you found success. The idea is that we want them to connect with you which will make them start to trust you. At the end of the email, you want to casually leave your link to your product/service.

**Day Three:** In the third email, this is where you carry on your story, but this is the point you had your epiphany – where everything clicked for you. Then, you would link the story to your product at the end.

**Day Four:** In the fourth email, this is where you list some of the benefits of your product/service but also listing some of the hidden benefits you did not realise at first.

**Day Five:** In the last of our sequence, we want to create urgency, so the reader must make a decision to take advantage before the price goes up.

After they have gone through our 5-day email campaign, we want to continue to send them daily emails to nurture that relationship and trust. If you do not email them every day, you will soon get replaced by someone else and by doing so, you are leaving a lot of money on the table.

Having an email list is the biggest asset you can as you own the traffic and do not have to fully rely on paid or organic traffic visiting your products and services. By nurturing and treating your email list well, you can continue to sell to the same people for years to come.

<u>Task</u>

1) Create a Lead Magnet that solves a common problem.

2) Set up your Lead Generation Funnel

3) Set up your 5 Email Marketing Campaign emails

(You can check out my Recommendations for your Lead Generation Funnel and Email Marketing Tool by going https://www.21daystolaunch.com/resourcespage)

# Day 4

## Your Hangout

So far, we have our Lead Generation Funnel and Emails all set up so we can start capturing peoples email addresses to do our email marketing but where should we place it? One of the best places to capture emails is to put it on your personal Facebook page.

You might be saying, well how do I get people to click on my profile in the first place? Good question! Do you remember the Facebook Groups where your Avatars are currently residing? You want to join as many as possible and provide amazing value in the form of posts and answering any questions people may have without selling yourself – the idea here is to be seen as an expert in your field so people click on your profile to see what you are all about.

Next up, you want to "advertise" your lead magnet in your Facebook cover photo and featured image (you can do this easily in Canva.com). Then, you want to put the link to your lead generation in the comments section of the photo.

Once they have opted into your lead magnet and landed on your thank you page, you then want to direct them to your own personal

Facebook group where they can access their freebie – they will also get their freebie sent to their email just to make sure.

Your own hangout is so important to build a community which allows you to test your market with your products and services to see what works and what does not. (More on that later)

Once they land on your "join group page", they will need to fill in some questions before you grant them access – we can acquire their email address again if they found your group through another way and add it manually to our email list. We can also find what kind of prospect they are for our services too.

Once they are in, you need to make sure your group is the best resource for their needs. You want to provide value every single day and go LIVE once a week to answer any questions and teach a certain topic.

## Facebook Messenger Client Method

To get clients through your Facebook Messenger, you want to be seen as a person of authority in your group. You want to add them as a friend to make sure they see all your posts and LIVES in the future to further build that trust.

During your lives where you are teaching a certain topic - offer a Lead Magnet in the form of a cheat-sheet or e-book of everything you just taught in the live so they can look at it for future reference.

You would ask them to comment #keyword to claim their lead magnet and then you would send it over to them through their Facebook Messenger. By doing this way, you open a dialogue where you can ask questions to find out if they are suitable for your services and get them on a free consultation call to discuss their needs.

## Grow your Hangout quickly using Paid Ads?

If you want to grow your Facebook group quickly, you can use paid advertising – you can send paid traffic to your Lead Generation funnel and direct them to join your hangout – this way of growing your email list and Facebook group is becoming more and more popular with coaches and consultants but if you do not know your market just yet then I would advise against it for the time being.

### Task
1) **Change your Facebook personal profile so you can funnel organic traffic to your private group.**
2) **Join as many groups as possible your avatar is hanging out and provide amazing value in them everyday**

3) Create your own hangout and have your questions set up at the front door.

4) Provide value in your hangout every day to build your tribe of followers.

# Day 5

## Your Show

We have our Lead Generation funnel set up to build an audience and we have a Facebook group for our loyal tribe of followers. Now we want to create our own show to build up credibility and take people on a journey. We do that in the shape of a Podcast.

Podcasts are becoming more and more popular in today's world, pretty much everyone listens to a podcast in one form or another. They listen to them while they are driving, while they are at work, in the bath, at the gym, while they go sleep. Etc.

Did you know a new podcast gets uploaded every 30 seconds? That is crazy which just shows you people love that kind of content – the kind of content where people can do two things at once and not have to sit down and stare at a screen. Podcasts are the easiest platform for someone to build trust which is why you should be starting a podcast today.

## What do you need?

Now you do not need any fancy equipment to get started. As you gain momentum then you can start looking at better quality stuff but right now, it is not needed. All you need is a mobile phone, app store and earphones with a mic built in.

Typically, podcasts have a 15 second trailer which tells the listener what the podcast is all about – have a listen to podcasts in your niche to see how theirs starts. You can create a 15 second trailer easily with mobile phone apps these days but if you want a more professional one, then look no further than fiverr.com.

Once you have your trailer done, you will want to record an intro with a hook that hooks in the listener, so they must listen to the whole episode.

And lastly, the main bit of content. Some people struggle to talk about a topic for 10 minutes but as time goes on, you will get better, and it will become natural.

If you are not sure what to talk about then document your journey up until that moment. Talk about your strengths, your worries, what you expect from the future etc. It does not matter what you say as such, as long as people can connect with your message then you can build an audience.

Once you have finished recording, you want to make sure your trailer is in the middle of your intro and main content – you can do this using an app and then you want to upload it to buzzsprout.com where they will upload it on all the podcast streaming sites such as Spotify, Amazon Music, Apple Music, etc.

The best thing about podcasts, let us say, you have done over 100 episodes, people who have just found you will go back to your very first episode to see how it all started which gives them hope that they can achieve similar results – the idea here is to be an inspiration to people so they come to you to use your services because you are the expert.

## Task

1) Create your Podcast and upload two shows a week for best results

2) Inform your Facebook Group and your Email List.

# Day 6

## Hacking

One of the most important things you must do is to see what your Dream 100 are currently doing to attract leads and how they sell their products/services. What we can do is "Funnel Hack" them – popular term coined by Russell Brunson.

The idea is to learn what our Dream 100 are doing with their ads, funnels, products, emails etc to see how they run their business so we can model our approach around theirs – if it is working for them, then it should work for us right?

Scroll through your Facebook News Feed and you should see ads targeting you in your niche. Look for the ones who have got the most engagement such as likes and comments. And have a look to see how old the comments are - the older the comments, the more success they must be getting from that ad.

Once you have found them, you will want to screenshot/screen capture their ads including their video ads to see the hooks they are using to lure people in and what kind of language they are using.

Next up, you want to screenshot/screen capture their landing page to see what kind of products they are selling and how they are selling it with their copy (the text) and images.

Sign up to their lead magnets and buy their low ticket offers using a new email address specially for this purpose – this will be our email swipe file so we can see how they maintain and nurture their audience to sell their products and services through their email marketing.

Once you have gone through their checkout, continue to "funnel hack" and you will be greeted by some "one time only" offers until you get to their thank you page. Once you are done, put that file into a separate Funnel Hacking folder for future reference. The reason for all this, is so that when we get to creating our product funnels in the future, we know exactly what is working and what is not.

Whenever you see an ad that you think is doing well, "funnel hack" it. The idea here is not to steal their copy (text), it is to take what works and put our own spin on it.

### Task
1) **Create a separate folder on your phone and computer for your funnel hacking swipes**
2) **Create a new email address for your email swipe file**
3) **Funnel hack your competitions successful ads**

# Day 7

## Breaking Even

So far, we have got the foundations for getting organic traffic nailed down – we are using the Facebook group method to gain followers and those followers are entering our Lead Generation funnel to get our daily emails. We have also got a podcast up and running giving more valuable content to our audience and everything is ticking along nicely.

For some people, this is enough but for others, me included - this is not quick enough. So, it is nearly time to use paid ads to scale our business quickly, but we do not have an awful lot of money to do it.

What we need to do is to duplicate our Lead Generation Funnel and add some steps to it to make a break-even funnel – we need to sell an informative product such as a video course in the range of $27-$97.

This product is called a Self-Liquidating Offer which self-liquidates our ad spend allowing us to grow our email list for free and scale our business quickly.

Our Self-Liquidating Offer must solve a deeper problem that is related to our Lead Magnet otherwise people are not going to be interested.

For example,

**Lead Magnet** - "Facebook Ads Swipe File" Swipe File

**Self-Liquidating Offer** - "How to Run a Successful Facebook Ad that scales your Business Quickly" Video Course - $37 (Usually $127)

When creating your Self-Liquidating Offer, your product does not have to be a fully fleshed out course - if it solves the problem, it can be as short as you want as some people want the solution right there and then. When outlining the structure of your course, make sure you lay out the steps to take your avatar with their "problem holding them back" to their "problem solved." Once you have it mapped out, start recording in order and upload it to a membership hosting platform or put it in a downloadable file.

You do not need any fancy equipment to create a course – just some screen capturing software, a phone and google slides will suffice for now.

# Task

Come up with the outline of your course that solves a deeper problem your avatar is facing and use it as your Self-Liquidating Offer.

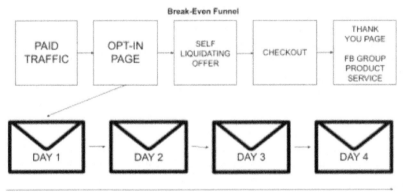

# Day 8

## Affiliate Marketing

Right, so we have come to the part that is one of my favourite ways to make a passive income and that is through Affiliate Marketing – this is where you promote a product or service for a commission. I make it sound so easy by saying that, but it is trickier than you think. Back in the day, you could send paid traffic to affiliate products and you would be raking it in but nowadays, people have wised up to that technique and most affiliate marketers have had to find something else to make money online.

The way to make affiliate marketing work these days is to use it in your teachings. I first started making affiliate commissions by teaching people how to use a product/service that solves the problem they had. And this is exactly what you should be doing in your Lead Magnet's and Self-liquidating products.

Find an Affiliate Product that can make your audience's lives easier and show them how to use it to great success. You can find affiliate products pretty much everywhere just by typing into google "product name" followed by "affiliate program." Just sign up and it is that easy!

The best affiliate products you can find are the ones that pay monthly commissions – these are usually service providers. They will pay you every month for however long that person stays signed up to that service – the great thing is that I am still getting paid by the same promotion I did three years ago!

They say to become a millionaire, you need to have at least 6 streams of income and Affiliate Marketing can be one of yours too.

## Task
**Find Affiliate Products to be a part of your Course to make Commissions.**

# Day 9

## Copywriting

Now here comes the tricky part, selling your products. What we need to understand is copywriting - this is the text you see on ads, emails and sales pages that try to make the viewer perform a specific action such as buy now. This is the hardest skill to master but if you can get good at it then it can literally make you millions.

The first thing we need to create is our Sales Page – on this page we can have a short, long or a video sales letter that basically goes through what the product is, its benefits, testimonials and lastly a call to action to buy. Now if you recommended a product to a friend, the chances are they would buy it off your recommendation because they would be classed as a warm lead.

However, our sales page will be directed at cold traffic, people who do not know who you are and have no reason to trust you just yet. That is why we create an engaging sales letter that targets their inner struggles and wants so they feel they must buy our solution to their problem.

Let me go through some of the elements of a sales page are. The first thing you will see is a big headline. The point of the headline is to sum up the main benefit of your product in one sentence which creates curiosity.

**"How to write and publish a book (in less than a week) without having to type a single word!"**

Below our headline will be either be a video sales letter or a written sales letter – they pretty much follow the script and pattern.

In the body of our text, we will have bullet points that list the benefits of our product to create even more curiosity.

- Build curiosity **so** you can make people want your solution to their problem.
- Grab people's attention **so** you can pinpoint their wants (and needs) to make more sales.
- Release important information quickly **so** you can get your message across fast to create impulse buying.

You see how I used bullet points to explain this topic and that is exactly what you can do on your sales page.

To really understand what a sales page is and how they flow, look back at your Funnel Hacking folder to see how your Dream 100 are presenting their products and model your sales page around theirs.

**<u>Task</u>**

**Create your Sales Page.**

**(TIP: Go to** https://www.21daystolaunch.com/resourcespage **to see my recommendation for a Copy Script Generator)**

# Day 10

## Testimonials

As part of your Sales Page or any product you sell, you should have Testimonials but when you are starting out, the chances are you will not have any. I am going to show you what you can do for now to use instead and how to get testimonials in the future. I will add right now before I start, do not fake results as it will only come back to bite you and if the authorities find out then you could be in for some trouble.

So, here is what you need to do to give some credibility to your product. Instead of providing fake results, use statistics to back up your product. If you are selling Search Optimization Services, then use stats around that.

**e.g., "72% of online marketers describe content marketing as their most effective SEO tactic."**

By providing statistics to back up what you are saying, you are making the reader believe you know what you are talking about and that your product is the solution – "if statistics back it, then it must be true."

# Getting Testimonials

So how do we get Testimonials for our sales page? This is where we get help from our Facebook Group (which you have been providing amazing value to everyday already).

You want to provide a high value post on your Self-liquidating offer topic in your hangout. You then tell your audience you are producing a course that solves that problem and you are giving it away to the first 10 people for free – if they want it, they must use a #keyword in the comments and you will send it them via their Facebook Messenger.

You would open a dialogue with them through Messenger and send them the product. After a few days, you want to check in to see how they are progressing. If they love it, ask if they can post it in the Facebook group for everyone to see - screenshot their glowing review and feature it on your Sales Page.

The quicker you get testimonials on your sales page, the quicker and higher your conversions will be.

## TASK
**1) Find statistics to back up your Self-Liquidating Product**
**2) Use your Facebook group to get Testimonials**

# Day 11

## Bonuses

So, now, you think your Self-Liquidating Offer is going to sell and you will get your money back no problem - that is a good belief to have but sometimes people are not ready to commit to your product just yet and they need gently persuading - we do this by offering a bonus stack that compliments your offer.

Bonuses can be anything that you would think would benefit your avatar and address any concerns they might have - this can be training, an audiobook, a cheat sheet, a pdf plan, done 4 u campaigns, a tool etc.

The idea is to woo our avatar with all these amazing bonuses that they feel they have no choice but to buy – without a bonus stack, the chance of you selling your product is low.

Next up, we need to work out how much are our bonuses are worth and how much we should charge. The best way is to follow the 10x model.

For example, say your Self-Liquidating offer is *"How to Run a Successful Facebook Ad"* and you value it at $37, you want to have all your bonuses add up to at least $377.

When coming up with your Bonuses, they need to be relevant to your offer and challenge any doubts your avatar might have. Let us say, if a customer loves the idea of using your product to help run their Facebook ads successfully but they their biggest doubt is that they are going to struggle coming up with the copy for their ad because writing is not their strongest skill. To eliminate that doubt we can add Ad Copy Generator software as a Bonus to sweeten the deal which makes them more inclined to purchase our product.

And the last bonus is usually something they cannot get anywhere else – this can be access to a private Facebook group or one to one call where they can ask you questions directly.

**Here is what's Included!**

**"How to Run A Successful Facebook Ad - $37".**

**"Ad Copy Generator Software - $127"**

**"Facebook Ads Cheat-sheet - $97"**

**"Facebook Ads Swipe File - $77"**

**"Done 4 You Facebook Ad Template - $67".**

**"Access to a Private Facebook Group - Priceless"**

**Total Value = $405      Get it all for <u>$37!</u>**

Come up with 5 Bonuses you can create that compliments your SLO.

# Day 12

## Your First Ad

Now the part people do not like, where they must put their money when their mouth is. Running paid ads. So, I am going to show the three steps in creating a successful ad and when you break it down, they are quite easy to do, the problem is we must create a lot.

In every successful ad whether it is an image ad, or a video ad is that it has an "attention grabber" to grab the right person. We can do this by using emotion, talking about payoffs, pains, worries, outcomes and obstacles, etc.

**E.g.**
**"Five Marketing Strategies every Consultant needs.**
**Five ways to market your consultancy business so you can get more clients on autopilot and not have to resort to cold calling. Click here now!"**

By using an attention grabber, we can grab the right people straight away and not have to waste money on the wrong people.

The second step to a successful ad is creating "curiosity" – we want people to question it and think how is this possible?

**"Want to get more."**
**"Want more."**
**"Want a higher return on your investment? "Want to have more time to do what you want?"**

By creating curiosity, it opens the thought process of them wanting your solution and are waiting for you to tell them on how they can get it which leads us to the third step – the "call to action."

This is where we tell the reader what to do if they want to find out more.

**"Five Marketing Strategies every Consultant needs to get more clients on autopilot without wasting time doing depressing cold outreach. Click here now."**

When you come up with your ads, make sure they follow the three-step formula otherwise your ads will just fail – this works for both text and video ads. (Tip: Video Ads have higher conversions as they build trust quicker)

## Task

Create a minimum of three ads with different copy, script, images or video.

# Day 13

## Testing

Most small businesses who fail at Facebook Advertising are not doing the basics - they run one or two ads and wonder why nothing is working so they end up stopping the campaign and have the belief that Facebook Ads is a waste of time and money.

The number one thing you must do when it comes to creating Ads is to test, test, test. You need to create different ads with different images and copy and test it against different audiences to find your winning ad - it is all about trial and error.

For example, let us say you are a supermodel, and you are in a photoshoot all day - the photographer will take hundreds of photos to find the perfect one that captures everything they want for their release - it is the same principle with your Paid Advertising. You need to go through the rubbish to find the one that resonates with your audience best.

Now I have created ads that I thought were amazing that resonated with me but did not with the audiences I was targeting. I have also had ads that I thought were bad and they turn out to be the best converting ones. My point is even if you think you know your market inside and out, you need to test a bunch of ads to see which one strikes a chord with them best. After three days of testing your ads, you want to stop the ones that are not performing and scale the ones that are.

## Lead Magnet/SLO Not Converting

So, you are getting traffic to your offer but no-one's biting - do not worry, this is normal. You need to change various bits on your offer page such as the image or the text - simply changing the headline can do wonders.

Now to make your life easier, some funnel builders can do A/B Testing on their landing pages which means they automatically switch between two to identify which one is performing best.

To do this, duplicate your landing page and change the headline so you have two slightly different landing pages - send traffic to both and after you have received a minimum of 1000 views on each page, you will be able to work out which landing page is performing best.

Once you have found the best landing page out of the two, duplicate the winning one and change other aspects such as the copy to see if it performs any better - the idea is to keep testing your landing pages until you know that page cannot be improved any further.

(Go to https://www.21daystolaunch.com/resourcespage to see my recommendation for A/B Testing landing pages)

## Ads No Longer Performing

After a while, your paid ads will not have the same effect as they once did as you are promoting to the same people who have already seen it so you will need to create more ads and test new audiences and markets - it is a never-ending process!

TIP: Take advantage of Google's $100/£75 ad credit for YouTube ads to start testing your video ads.

<u>**Task**</u>

**Create Ad Campaigns to test different audiences to see which ads come out on top.**

# Day 14

## Profiting

So, now we have our Break-even funnel up and running and we are currently in the testing stage of our ads and landing page. What we need to do now is to add more products so we can make our Break-even funnel profitable – we can do this by creating upsells.

The first upsell we can create is called an Order Bump which you will see on the checkout of most online stores – this is the same idea such as going to a store and the cashier tries to get you to add something to your basket. "Would you like to add a Mars Bar for just $1 to your order?" It is the same principle.

By adding an Order Bump, you can identify who the hyperactive buyers are and then you can send them emails directly to them to encourage them to buy more of your products/services - order bumps are generally priced between $7-$47.

The next upsell we can offer is called a One Time Only offer - an offer they will not see anywhere else. After someone has purchased your self-liquidating offer and gone through your checkout, they are taken to a "One Time Only" offer page. On this page, you can offer another product or course that is closely related to your Self-Liquidating offer that solves a bigger problem.

The great thing about these pages is that they do not require the customer to go through the checkout stage again – they just have to click "add to order" and it comes out their bank account straight away - these can be priced from anywhere from $47 to $497.

If the customer does not want your offer, they are then directed to a down-sell offer - this can be the same product, but with a payment plan over a period of months or you can sell a completely different product. By having a down-sell page, you are giving yourself more chance of closing that sale and making more money.

Another type of upsell we can add to our funnel is called the Profit Maximiser – this is where you offer a "membership" where you add more in-depth lessons on different topics, adding regular content and keeping up to date with the times. By charging a monthly fee, then you are getting a recurring income from your members which means you open another stream of income.

When setting up the tiers to your membership, make sure you have three different levels. The first one should be a monthly plan such as $37 a month (cancel anytime). The second should be a 12-month membership plan which you charge 10x the price of your monthly plan such as $397 and the third one should be a lifetime membership with a heavy discount where you can charge $497.

By offering different prices, you are giving the option to your customers – some people would rather test the water by getting the monthly plan and see how it goes and others want to save money in the long run and will purchase the bigger plans.

Now there is no limits to the amount of upsells you can add to your funnel however, I would suggest no more than three offers otherwise you are going to annoy your customers going through all these deals which will not do you any good with your audience long term.

After they have gone through your upsells, they are taken to a thank you page where you can display your affiliate recommendation, booking schedule form for a free consultation call or direct them to your Facebook group.

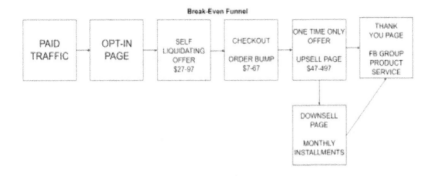

## Task

Create upsells to make your Break-Even Funnel profitable.

# Day 15

## Infiltrating

So, every day, you have been watching how your Dream 100 have been engaging with their audience, what type of posts are they doing, their ads, emails, etc. Well, due to your liking and commenting on all their stuff, it will now stand you in good stead when you do message them. This is because they will recognize your face and name when you pop up in their inbox and be more inclined to message you back, so it is essential you get your first message right - do not send a templated message that you send to everyone.

Your message needs to be personal to them - talk about their interests such as their family, music, art etc. And most importantly, do not talk about yourself - this is not about you, it is all about them.

After 30 days onwards, you want to make your Dream 100 love what you do. You can do this by sending them free access to your course, product or service. Then, they will share you to their audience and you will gain followers - this is where you can ask them to be featured on your Podcast, YouTube Channel or Facebook Group Live for an interview and vice versa.

The key to all this, is to follow as many of your Dream 100 as possible as it really is a numbers game. At the start, most of your competition will not trust you so it is important to put the foundations in and build that relationship first then in that way you will start seeing more yeses and getting less no's when you do ask for a favour.

## Task

**Message your Dream 100 a personalized message to start a conversation.**

# Day 16

## Product Research

Now if you have a big enough Facebook group size then I would recommend doing this before you create your Self-Liquidating offer however if you find that your self-liquidating offer is still not converting, then you might have an issue with your product – maybe people are just not interested in it – it happens…. a lot

So, we need to do some market research, we need to use our Facebook group to see what they want to learn from you that will solve their problems – we do this by creating a survey/questionnaire and get them to fill it in with as much detail as possible. We want them to list down their struggles, worries and current beliefs that is stopping them from achieving success. By doing this, it gives us better information about our avatar for sales letters and ad copy.

Once they have filled it in, we can then analyse the data and see what content they want and get down to creating it. We can also use the exact phrasing and words they use in their answers as part of our sales letters in the future – this is the best way to really understand your customers and how to connect to their internal struggles to make sales.

Before you create any product in the future, you should be researching if your product idea is something people want – research your market by asking your own Facebook group.

### Task

**Create a Survey/Form so you can identify the problems your audience want solving, then outline your course around their answers and create it.**

# Day 17

## Affiliates

For us to get our name out there further and make more money, we can set up an affiliate program on our funnels. We want people to promote our funnel on their blogs, email lists, YouTube, etc to get further reach and in return they make affiliate commissions.

First thing you want to do is create promotional items such as lead magnets, banners, and sample emails for them to use in their email marketing campaigns - give them anything that you think would be useful to promote your product.

Next up we want to find affiliates - you can find them by contacting people who have already purchased your products. You can send your product for free to your dream 100 so they can recommend you to their list. You can message Blogs/YouTube owners and send them a copy to review on their platform.

Also, you will find people often coming to you and ask if they can promote your product because they love it so much but some of them do not know how to promote it exactly. Teach them how to promote it properly with a series of tutorials going through step by step on the different methods.

If you form an Affiliate Army for your business, then there is no telling on how far your product can go.

**Task – Set up Affiliate Programs for your Funnels and create promotional products/samples.**

# Day 18

## V.I.P. Only

In our Facebook Group, we have been providing value every day and going Live once a week teaching and answering questions.

We have learnt the ways on how to acquire their email address for our email marketing and we have learnt how to prospect them to see if they are a suitable client to get on a free consultation call.

Now, we want to monetise our whole group – we do this through a V.I.P Masterclass that we advertise only to our Facebook Group – you tell your audience you have a special V.I.P Masterclass happening in 2-4 weeks' time that will show them step by step on how to solve their problem fast.

You would leave your link to the registration page where they can pay for a seat for your masterclass. On the next page, you would then add them to another private Facebook group, and you would send them daily emails along with email reminders to attend the class.

Then, you would perform your masterclass Live to your audience and answer any questions they may have.

After your live show, you want to screenshot all the comments and use them as your testimonials in your Facebook Group and tell all your Facebook Group how successful it was – this will make people feel like they missed out and will not want to miss out on the next masterclass.

Alternatively, you could add a replay masterclass for those who missed it and direct them to a replay registration page to make more money.

V.I.P. masterclasses are becoming more popular on Facebook and many charge at least $47 to attend – often is the case they have at least 200 people in them at a time – that is $9,400 in one night!

## Task
**Outline your Masterclass Idea and Advertise it to your Facebook Group regularly**

# Day 19

## Better than a Business Card

If you want to get high ticket clients and be the authority figure in your niche, then you need to write a book - now hear me out. A book establishes you as an expert in your field and builds that level of trust that no other format can match. It can open doors to interviews on popular podcasts, blogs, YouTube channels and even speaking jobs to further your portfolio.

And I know exactly what you are saying right now, I do not have the time to sit at my desk writing a book - well you can write a book in a day without even typing a single word - sounds strange right?

And you also might be saying, I do not have all the knowledge just yet to write a 200+ page book. My answer to that is, your book can be any length as long as it solves the problem.

## Timeline

The steps that I am going to lay out to write your book are quite simple as anyone can do this if they know their field well.

First step is to take a piece of paper and turn it landscape – draw a big line going through the middle with a happy face and a sad face on each end – this is going to be our timeline.

Now what is your book all about? What problem is it solving? You need to come up with the relevant steps that will take your unhappy person away from their problem and turn them into a happy one with their problem solved - these steps will become the chapters in your book.

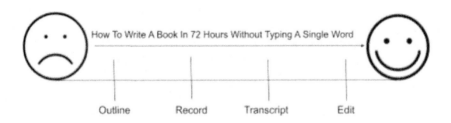

Outline    Record    Transcript    Edit

## Quadrants

Once you have outlined the steps of your timeline, you then want to get another piece of paper and split it into four quadrants - these quadrants represent your chapters.

Next, you want to break down each step (quadrant) into 5 points explaining how to do that step.

When you are writing your bullet points you want to make sure you are focusing on the big picture and not getting side-tracked.

And make sure you have some sort of story element (your experience) so that people can connect with you and feel they can achieve the same.

| Outline | Record |
|---|---|
| - Timeline<br>- Quadrant<br>- 5 Points per Quadrant<br>- Focus on Big Picture<br>- Story | |
| Transcript | Edit |
| | |

# Record

Next up, we want to create a PowerPoint presentation so we can use it as a guide when we record our voice explaining the chapters in our book – each slide represents a quadrant. We want to put our bullet points down here and any notes we feel would be useful to talk about.

Once you are ready to go, record your voice using your mobile phone and talk about each point for 2-5 minutes. If you speak for 2 minutes on each point, you will have at least 40-60 minutes of audio which transcribe to about 60 pages for your book which is plenty to acquire customers.

# Transcript & Edit.

Next up, you want to take your Audio, and have it transcribed into a text format using rev.com - they will get your transcription done quickly and at a cheap price.

Once you have received your transcript back, do not look at it, it is going to look terrible. We need to have someone proofread and edit it, so it is ready for release - go to Fiverr.com and get it done for a reasonable price.

Next, we need to format our book, and this is where we use our good friends at Fiverr again - find someone who has good reviews and is priced reasonably.

## Releasing Your Book

Once your book is formatted, you can upload it to Amazon Kindle Direct Publishing - this will be automatically listed on Amazon and they will print and ship your book whenever someone orders it.

They also pay up to 70% royalties on your sales which is great although make sure you select the agreement that allows you to sell your book on other platforms - this is important if we are going to sell it through our marketing strategy.

If you do not like Amazon and what they stand for (some people do not) you can use Print-On-Demand Publishing Services such as Lulu or Ingram-spark.

## Free+Shipping

We have our brand spanking new book ready, and our physical copy is on its way to us – how do we get high ticket clients with it?

We give it away.... sort of.

We give it away, but we ask the customer to pay for the postage and packaging – this technique is one of the most powerful ways to get high ticket clients coming into your business.

The power of the word "Free" and getting something physical in return makes your content valuable – people value physical books higher than a pdf file. By giving a physical book away you are seen as the ultimate figure of authority and when they read your book, they will see you as the solution to their problems and contact you.

So how do we give it away?

We give it away in a Tripwire Funnel – now this is like our Break-Even Funnel but instead of our Self-Liquidating product, we replace it with it our book.

By going down the Free + Shipping route, you will lose money to start with due to advertising costs, but you will make it back and gain so much more with your upsells, email marketing and people enquiring to use your services after reading your book.

Alternatively, you could sell your book as an e-book instead for $7 and use it as a self-liquidating offer however it will not have the same client pulling effect as doing the Free + Shipping method.

**Example of acquiring a Customer using Paid Ads (updated)**

So, here is the ad costs to acquire one person to buy my "21 Days to Launch" book in 2020.

The postage and packaging price for my book was $7.95. I spent about $23 to acquire one customer of the book which meant we were down by $14.05.

Now we had an order bump on the checkout offering a mini-course loosely related to the book for $37 and 19% of the customers added it to their order - now we are still down by -$8.15 to acquire one customer.

Now comes the upsell with our core offer which teaches them on how to achieve faster results, priced at $97. Now 11% of customers ended up adding that to their order and now we are making $1.87 per customer which is growing our email list for free – this is what we want so we can continue to promote our offers and products with our email marketing which is a powerful asset to have.

Then we sold a further upsell of $297 and about 3% added that to their order and now we are making a profit of $10.12 for each customer who progressed through our funnel.

And then on the thank you page, I had a video demonstrating why they should use my services and to book an appointment to speak to one of my team members.

As you can see, we are making about $10 for every $1 we spend on advertising which is a fantastic return on investment – this does not include the people who buy the book through our email list and Facebook group either.

Before you send paid traffic to your book funnel, use traffic from your Facebook group and email list to see how well your page converts.

If you are a Coach or Consultant, then writing and marketing your book using the Free+Shipping Model will get you higher ticket clients for your business.

### Task

**Write a book using the steps outlined to pull in high ticket clients.**

**When you have the budget, sell your book using the Free + Shipping Model.**

# Day 20

## Prospecting Your List

So, people are signing up to your email list, but we do not actually know if they require our services. We could ask for their mobile number when they sign up to our lead magnet or SLO which is good to start with, but it can be a pain ringing up people and getting "sorry, not interested" - might do your confidence in.

We want to target people on our email list who are needing our solution to their problem, so we can create a Prospector Funnel for our email list. The idea is to take our existing leads and then send them to a Demonstration Page where we talk about our services and how we can help them — include testimonials and case studies.

During our video demo, a call-to-action button will appear on the video asking if they are ready to start their journey. If they do not click the button, they get added to a follow up email sequence which sends a reminder email every two days to return to the demo page to start their journey. If they do click the call-to-action button, they are taken to a thank you page where they can book an appointment to speak to you.

Shortly after they are directed to a pre-survey form where you can prospect them with questions to find out if they would be a good fit for your business thus saving you so much time.

This type of funnel is one of the most important funnels for my social media advertising business as I do not have to hire a bunch of staff to ring up people as the clients come to me wanting my services. You can add this type of funnel to your conclusion section of your book too where you can promote your services.

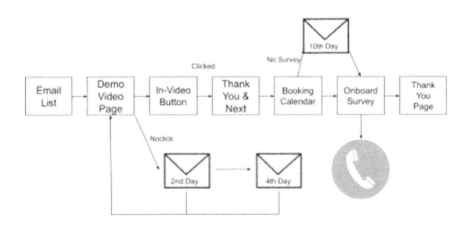

<u>Task</u>

**Set up Prospector Funnel and create a Demo Video of your Services (include Testimonials and Case Studies)**

# 21 Days and Beyond

So, you now know the foundations to your business, and you have the knowledge to scale your business fast - you do not have to follow all the steps down to a tee but look at it as a guide so you can track your progress.

Just be confident in the fact that you can do it and with a little bit of hard work and time management, you can build a successful business.

Just do not forget your roots and always continue to nurture and take care of your email list - without it, you will be back to square one.

Once this book is available, I know it is going to be difficult to accommodate everyone who wants my personalized help. So, I created something incredibly special for the readers of this book.

I have opened space up in the 21 Days and Beyond program where my team will launch your course, coaching and consulting business from the ground up – we literally handle everything such as the creation of your funnels, paid ads with all the copy, hire and train a sales team to close sales calls so you can just focus on what you do best and that is creating the content and enjoying life.

To be considered, then visit the link below, and fill in the application, and my team will contact you to see if we are a good fit or not. If we are then my team will arrange with you an hour-long phone call with myself to come up with a personalized strategy for your business and then my team will help you implement the changes over the next 12 months. You can apply here:

https://www.21daysandbeyond.com

Just think, in less than a week, we could be talking to each other on the phone (re)launching your business!

Thank you so much for reading and I wish you great success on your journey!

Daniel Steed

# Dan's Recommended Reading

Sell Like Crazy

By Sabri Suby


The Ultimate Sales Machine

By Chet Holmes


Traffic Secrets

By Russell Brunson


Dotcom Secrets

By Russell Brunson


Expert Secrets

By Russell Brunson


Copywriting Secrets

By Jim Edwards


Advertising Secrets of the Written Word

By Joe Sugarman

## About the Author

**Daniel Steed** started his first online company while looking after children in care. Within 12 months, he started making 4 figures a week using paid advertising promoting his Affiliate Marketing Products. After seeing the success his advertising methods were getting - he created *Social on Point* which has helped hundreds of people grow their business using paid advertising. He lives in Shrewsbury, United Kingdom and enjoys taking his dogs up the mountains on the weekends - you can find out more at socialonpoint.com.

Printed in Great Britain
by Amazon

77537471R00068